I0815537

Boston RED SOX

KENNY ABDO

An Imprint of Abdo Zoom
abdobooks.com

abdobooks.com

Published by Abdo Zoom, a division of ABDO, P.O. Box 398166, Minneapolis, Minnesota 55439.

Printed in the United States of America, North Mankato, Minnesota.
102025
012026

Photo Credits: AP Images, Getty Images, Shutterstock
Production Contributors: Kenny Abdo, Jennie Forsberg, Grace Hansen
Design Contributors: Candice Keimig, Neil Klinepier

Library of Congress Control Number: 2025936768

Publisher's Cataloging-in-Publication Data

Names: Abdo, Kenny, author.
Title: Boston Red Sox / by Kenny Abdo
Description: Minneapolis, Minnesota : Abdo Zoom, 2026 | Series: MLB teams | Includes online resources and index.
Identifiers: ISBN 9798384940128 (lib. bdg.) | ISBN 9798384940883 (ebook) | ISBN 9798384941262 (read-to-me ebook)
Subjects: LCSH: Boston Red Sox (Baseball team)--Juvenile literature. | Baseball teams--Juvenile literature. | Professional sports--Juvenile literature. | Sports franchises--Juvenile literature. | Major League Baseball (Organization)--Juvenile literature.
Classification: DDC 796.357--dc23

Table of CONTENTS

RED SOX

As one of the oldest **franchises** in Major League Baseball (MLB), the Boston Red Sox have experienced everything from clean victories to losses that stink!

With more than 120 years on the field and a roster of unforgettable players, the Red Sox have battled curses, won championships, and built an everlasting baseball **dynasty**.

BATTER UP!

Boston's baseball team began in 1901. First called the Americans, the team started strong and won the first World Series in 1903. Cy Young threw a no-hitter the next season. In 1908, the team became the Red Sox, named for the red stockings they wore.

BOSTON
51641

RED S

Babe Ruth started his career as a pitcher for the Red Sox in 1914. He ruled the mound, earning major **records** during the 1915 and 1916 seasons. Ruth was also a strong hitter, setting another record with 29 home runs in 1919. However, he was sold to the Yankees at the end of the 1919 season.

The **Curse of the Bambino** began after the sale of Ruth. For many years, the Red Sox had trouble winning. Though fans grew frustrated, they also came together. And they never lost hope!

RED SOX

GRAND SLAMS

In 1967, the "**Impossible Dream**" team, led by Carl Yastrzemski, reached the World Series. Although the Red Sox did not win, they reignited fans' love and brought new energy to the team.

In 1975, the Red Sox took another swing at the World Series. Excitement peaked when Carlton Fisk made his famous home run in Game 6. Although the Sox lost to the Reds, the thrill was unforgettable. Fisk's homer remains a moment Boston fans still talk about today.

In 2004, the Red Sox finally broke the **Curse of the Bambino**. With a historic comeback against the Yankees in the playoffs, the team **swept** the Cardinals in the World Series. The win marked the Red Sox's first championship in 86 years.

BOSTON

The Red Sox gained momentum, winning World Series titles in 2007, 2013, and 2018. However, the team lost steam in 2019. They finished with an 84–78 **record** and missed the playoffs.

2018
WORLD SERIES
CHAMPS

MassMutual
Boston

After losing to the Astros in the 2021 **American League (AL)** Championship Series, the Red Sox struggled. The team finished last in the AL East in 2022 and 2023 but climbed to third place in 2024. By 2025, rising stars like Wilyer Abreu gave fans hope through strong at-bats and solid defense!

HALL OF FAME

Ted Williams, known as the "Splendid Splinter," was a great hitter with a .406 average in 1941. He played his entire career with the Boston Red Sox and is considered one of the greatest batters of all time. Williams was **inducted** into the Baseball Hall of Fame in 1966.

TON

Carl Yastrzemski played his 23-year career with the Red Sox. He won the **Triple Crown** in 1967 and finished his career with 452 home runs and 3,419 hits. Yastrzemski was named to the Baseball Hall of Fame in 1989.

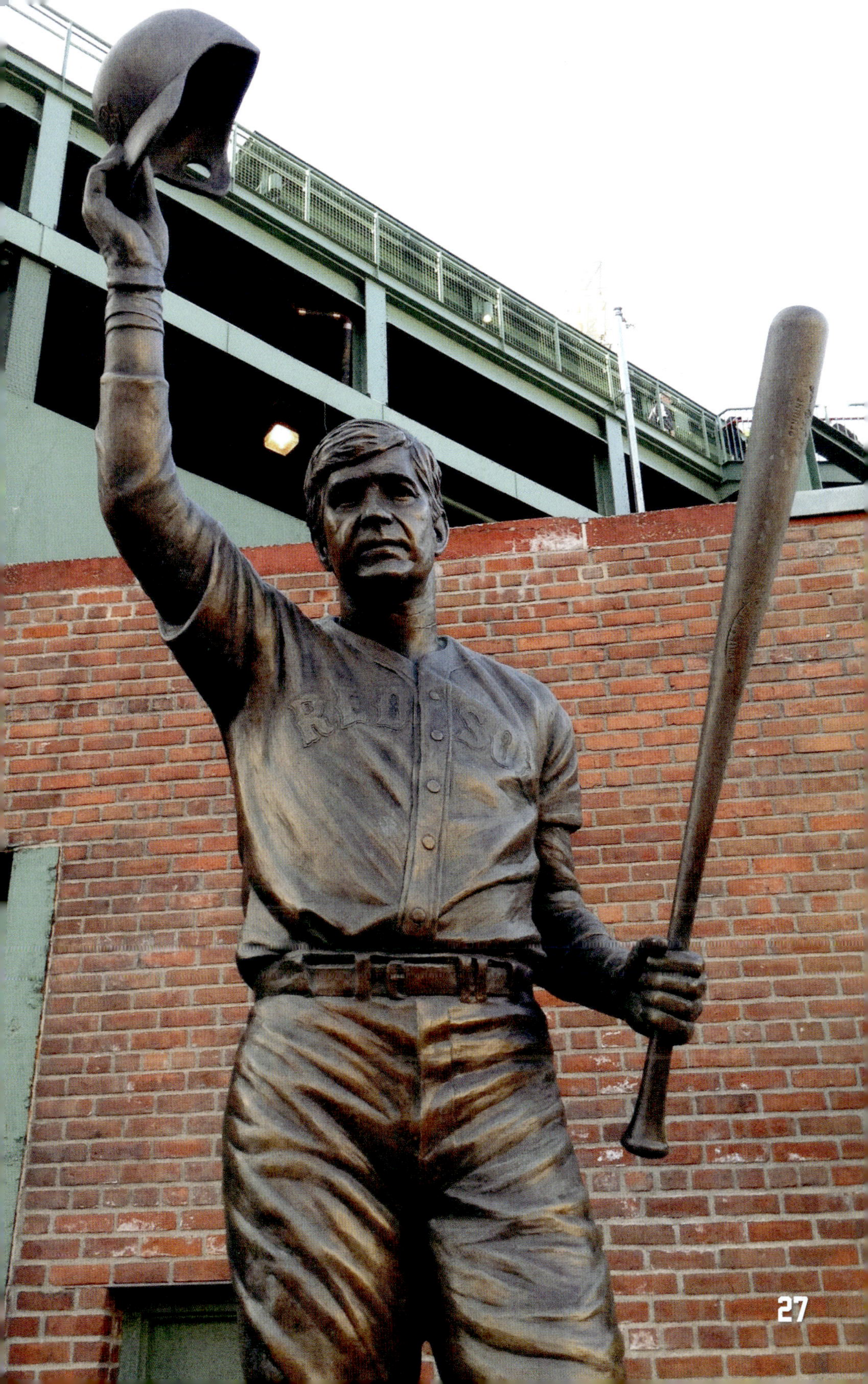

Wade Boggs was a star player on the Red Sox from 1982 to 1992. He had more than 2,200 hits and a batting average of .328. Boggs won five batting titles, played in 12 **All-Star Games**, and was known for his control at the plate. He entered the Baseball Hall of Fame in 2005.

BOGGS

GLOSSARY

All-Star Game – a yearly baseball contest where top players from the AL and the National League (NL) compete against each other.

American League (AL) – one of two 15-team leagues that make up MLB.

Curse of the Bambino – a superstitious curse that plagued the Boston Red Sox between 1918 and 2004. During this time, the team never won a World Series.

dynasty – a team that has an extended period of success, usually winning multiple championships in the process.

franchise – a sports organization, including the top-level team and all minor league affiliates.

Impossible Dream – the name for the 1967 season when the Red Sox achieved an improbable turnaround.

inducted – brought in as a member.

record – a team's season total of wins and losses; also a top achievement by a player or team that no one has done before.

swept – to have won all games in a series.

Triple Crown – the achievement earned when a pitcher leads the league in wins, strikeouts, and earned-run average in the same season.

ONLINE RESOURCES

To learn more about the Boston Red Sox, please visit **abdobooklinks.com** or scan this QR code. These links are routinely monitored and updated to provide the most current information available.

INDEX